I0159299

Salvation

God's Provision and our Response

Brian Sherring

ISBN: 978-1-78364-426-1

The Open Bible Trust
Fordland Mount, Upper Basildon,
Reading, RG8 8LU, UK.

www.obt.org.uk

Salvation

God's Provision and our Response

Contents

Preface

Preface

This booklet is not a theological treatise, but is an attempt to show there is much more involved in the Scriptural idea of 'salvation' than is generally believed. Some of the great truths that are involved in salvation can easily be missed and I want to look at some of them, in the hope that by doing so the work of Jesus Christ, our Saviour, may be more fully appreciated

The basic truth of salvation is enshrined in the words, "Believe in the Lord Jesus, and you will be saved" (Acts 16:31). It is childlike in its simplicity and surely not beyond the capability of any to grasp. I have endeavoured to keep this work, as far as possible, in the same simple vein, whilst looking at the meaning of 'salvation' in more of its fullness.

'Salvation' is not a word that is much used in everyday speech. As a subject, however, it runs like a silken thread through the Bible from beginning to end. From its earliest chapters, man's need for salvation is made plain and so also is God's provision to meet that need. This booklet looks at it from a number of angles that we hope will show that it is the most vital truth for us to understand and take hold of. In short, it is something that takes in every part of everyday life and will one day decide our future.

The Simple Facts

The Simple Facts

The Bible calls Jesus Christ a Saviour, that is, One Who saves. He is so named because He was sent by God to *save* us from the consequences of sin. All who have ever lived have been sinners and the punishment for sin is death. Jesus Christ was able to accept the punishment of death in our place, because He was not a sinner. On the third day after His death, He rose from the dead, proving that He had broken the power of death, as it was not able to hold Him. He was made alive again and through Him God now offers life to those who believe in Him. That life begins now and passes through resurrection into eternal life. We are asked to believe in Christ and trust in what He has done for us. We are called upon to accept that He died and rose again. By believing in Him we accept salvation and the life He offers.

Our need for a Saviour

The word 'sinner', as with the word 'salvation' does not figure much in everyday conversation, but God says that all are sinners. The Apostle Paul wrote in Romans chapter 3, verses 9 and 10, "Jews and Gentiles alike are all under sin. As it is written: 'There is no-one righteous, not even one'". Jews and Gentiles, in Biblical terms, encompass the whole human race; there is not one righteous person by God's standard. If we are honest we already know and accept this, as every word or action that our conscience tells us is wrong, is 'sin' by God's standard. Some may live 'good lives' and some 'bad lives' by human standards; in God's eyes all are sinners and in *need* of the salvation offered in Christ Jesus.

How did we all become Sinners?

Romans chapter 5 verse 19 answers this question:

> Through the disobedience of the one man the many were made sinners.

The 'one man' spoken of here is Adam, who disobeyed God's commandment in the Garden of Eden. The whole account may be read in Genesis chapters 2 and 3. Through disobedience Adam became a sinner and as all have descended from him, so all have inherited his sinful nature. Our relationship to the first man Adam has made us all sinners. But however unfair this may seem and not our fault, we should note that God condemns no one because of his relationship to Adam. We are judged by what we choose to be, when we either accept or reject God's offer of salvation in Christ that undoes the failure of Adam. More of this later, for now it is enough to see that **we are sinners because of our relationship to Adam.**

What does it mean to be a Sinner?

Sin subjects us to death

When Adam was created he was innocent, but he was warned against disobedience to God. God had said to him, "You are free to eat from any tree in the garden; but you must not eat from the tree of the knowledge of good and evil, for when you eat of it you will surely die" (Genesis chapter 2 verses 16, 17). By disobeying God's direct command Adam became a sinner and brought death, not only on himself, but also on all his descendants.

Like a hereditary disease, death passed down to all mankind. Although Adam lived to a great age, in the end he died, the consequence of his sin. See Genesis chapter 5 verse 5, "Altogether, Adam lived 930 years, and then he died".

None could be allowed to live forever as sinners. Death, however long it is delayed, is the final consequence of sin. The Bible views it as something that is earned, as Romans 6:23 puts it; "the wages of sin is death". **A sinner then is a person subject to death.** When "sin entered the world through one man" it brought death that was passed on to all men, for all are sinners. See Romans 5:12 where the "one man" in this verse is Adam.

Sin separates us from God

Before Adam sinned he lived in the Garden of Eden, a place where he was able to talk freely with God. When he became a sinner, however, he was driven out of the Garden and became *separated* from God. Genesis 3:23,24, "So the Lord God banished him from the Garden of Eden

… he drove the man out". **A sinner then is a person separated from God.**

Aspects of our Separation from God

There are a number of ways in which God speaks of this separation in the Bible. We are all looked upon as separated from God because:

(a) We are **unrighteous**
(b) We are **enemies of God**
(c) We are **servants of sin** and subject to death.
(d) We are **debtors**

This fourfold position demonstrates how great is our need of Christ and the salvation God offers us through Him. How then has God delivered us from this position of total separation from God and the death that will surely follow? Before we can answer this question we have to realise that God is different from us in one very important respect.

The Righteousness of God

Christ's sacrifice satisfies God's justice

God is righteous and cannot break His word or simply overlook sin. He has said, "The wages of sin is death"; sin must be paid for by death and it cannot be overlooked or simply forgotten about. If we cannot believe God's word about this, then we are without hope and we could not trust anything He said. He would not then be a righteous God or able to provide deliverance from the condemnation we are under as sinners. But He is the righteous God and has found a way by which His righteousness is not compromised and our deliverance is assured. That deliverance is made possible because Christ has paid the penalty for sin on our behalf. He died in our place. It was a substitution – a life for a life. "Christ died for our sins" (1 Corinthians 15:3). See also Romans 5:8.

> God demonstrates his own love for us in this: While we were still sinners, Christ died for us.

But Christ did not remain dead. If He had done so, then He would have been no different from others. It could have been claimed that, as with the rest of mankind, He died for His own sin. But He was sinless, so after three days He was made alive again: God raised Him from the dead. His resurrection proves that our sins have been fully paid for; God's justice is satisfied. Death could not hold Him; He has broken its power, so that we can now say,

> Death has been swallowed up in victory. "Where, O death, is your victory? Where, O death, is your sting?" (1 Corinthians 15:54,55)

God's justice is satisfied; sin is dealt with; the power of death is broken; in Christ the way is now open for our deliverance. What must we then do to be saved from sin and its consequence, death?

The Way
of
Salvation

The Way of Salvation

We have now only to believe in Him in order to be saved. It is as simple as that. Perhaps it is too simple for some, who feel that they have to do something; live good lives, go to church etc.

These things have their place later, but they have no place in the initial acceptance of *the all-sufficient work of Christ* on our behalf. We can add nothing to what He has done. It was once and for all. This is good news (the 'gospel') and this gospel is summed up in the words of Paul,

> For what I received I passed on to you as of first importance: that Christ died for our sins according to the Scriptures, that he was buried, that he was raised on the third day according to the Scriptures. (1 Corinthians 15:3,4)

To believe in Christ is to accept what He has done for us.

What it means, therefore, to be Saved

A sinner is a person subject to death. A sinner is a person separated from God. By nature we are all sinners so we are all subject to death and separated from God. Christ has died for our sins, broken the power of death and given us a promise of resurrection life.

> God so loved the world that he gave his one and only Son, that whoever believes in him shall not perish but have eternal life. (John 3:16)

First of all then, **to be saved means to be saved from death**. This does not mean that we will not die, but that death will not be able to hold us, we will be saved out of it. Death will not be victorious. Those who believe in Christ can now think of dying as though it means going to sleep. In 1 Corinthians 15:18 believers who have died are called, "those who have fallen asleep in Christ". As we are not afraid of going to sleep at night, being confident that we shall wake up in the morning, so is it for those who trust in Christ.

There is now no sting in death. Its fear should be gone. Our belief is that we shall wake up into resurrection life. Death has been made of no effect.

> Our Saviour, Christ Jesus, who has destroyed death and has brought life and immortality to light through the gospel. (2 Timothy 1:10)

The word "destroyed" here means 'brought to nothing'. Christ has broken the power of death so that it cannot hold us and therefore we need not fear it if we are trusting in Him. This is the certainty held out to us in salvation. Because we are sinners we are separated from God. Salvation ends that separation and brings us to God. So, secondly, **to be saved means to be no longer separated from God.**

> For Christ died for sins once for all, the righteous for the unrighteous, to bring you to God. (1 Peter 3:18)

| Christic has paid for sin |

Christ has paid for sin Christ has paid for the sin that separated us from God. That separation is now ended; He has brought us to God. We saw four ways that describe our separation from God. a) We are unrighteous; b) we are enemies of God; c) we are servants of sin, and d) we are debtors. Christ has dealt with every aspect of our separation from God, as we will now see.

Unrighteous: The Answer - Justification

We are looked upon as being separated from God because we are unrighteous. See 1 Peter 3:18 where we are called 'the unrighteous', which means the same as *unjust*. God's remedy through Jesus Christ is *justification*. If we accept Christ as the One who has dealt with sin, He looks upon us **as though we are** righteous, **as though we are** just. This does not mean that we are actually now sinless, righteous or just, simply that **we are looked upon as such**. Think of it like this. When I am justified it is JUST-AS-IF-I'D never sinned.

We must be clear about this. Justification does not mean that God has made us righteous, but that **He counts us** righteous. If God had made us righteous then we could no longer sin, which we know is not true, so we cannot have been made righteous. It is because God looks at us through Christ that He can count us righteous, and He counts our faith in Him for righteousness.

Romans chapter 4 gives us an example of a man who was looked upon by God as righteous. Verse 3 reads,

> Abraham believed God, and it was credited to him as righteousness.

All Abraham did was to *believe* God's promise. The whole story of Abraham's faith in God may be read in Genesis chapter 15, where verse 6 is the quotation used in Romans 4:3 above. Abraham was as much a sinner as anyone else, but because of his faith (he believed God) he **was looked upon as** righteous. His faith was credited or counted for righteousness. Reading on further in Romans chapter 4, verses 23-25, we see that Abraham was only one example of God's grace, a grace He offers to us also.

> The words 'it was credited to him' were written not for him alone, **but also for us**, to whom God will credit righteousness – for us who believe in him who raised Jesus our Lord from the dead. He was delivered over to death for our sins and was raised to life for our justification.

Abraham believed in the God who can bring life out of death. When we believe in Him as the One who raised the Lord Jesus Christ from the dead, then He counts that faith of ours for righteousness. He looks at us as though we are righteous. Now see Romans 5:1,

> Therefore, since we have been justified through faith, **we have peace with God** through our Lord Jesus Christ.

This verse suggests a second way in which we are separated from God and His remedy in Christ to end that separation.

Enemies: The Answer - Reconciliation

By nature we are enemies of God as Romans 5:10 says, "We were God's enemies". That enmity, or alienation, is identified for us in Colossians 1:21 where, looking back on his reader's pre-Christian days, Paul wrote,

> Once you were **alienated from God** and were **enemies** in your minds because of your evil behaviour.

We may feel that these words are rather hard on us and cannot fairly describe our way of life as unbelievers, but the enmity that is here spoken of is **in the mind**. It is what goes on in the mind that influences our way of life. Minds not in tune with God's will are at enmity with Him and, however good (in our eyes) our way of life may seem, it is not enough to bring us before Him without condemnation. God has provided the remedy, however, in Christ. The enmity has been broken down. Reconciliation has been made. Peace has been made between God and ourselves. We are no longer separated from Him. Reading further on in Romans 5, verse 10 tells us how God has done this:

> When we were God's enemies, we were reconciled to him **through the death of his Son.**

This verse goes on to show that since this reconciliation has taken place, the way is now open for our salvation,

> How much more, having been reconciled, shall we be saved through his life!

The importance of the death **and** resurrection of Christ cannot be too strongly emphasised. His death, which paid the wages of sin, allowed for our reconciliation, but if He had not overcome that death in resurrection, there could be no salvation; we shall be saved **by His life.**

An illustration of the meaning of reconciliation can be found in the story of the prodigal son in Luke 15:11-24; please read it. Reconciliation is one part of God's remedy to end the separation between us, so that we are no longer His enemies, separated from Him, but are at peace with God.

Servants of Sin: The Answer – Redemption

We are looked upon as separated from God because by nature we are servants of sin. Strictly speaking we should say slaves of sin, for a servant may leave his master, but we are bound like slaves to serve sin. By nature we have no option. See Romans 6:17 and note the words expressing what the Roman Christians were in time past,

> You used to be slaves to sin.

God's remedy to set us free from this condition of slavery to sin is **redemption** and is again made possible by the work of Christ on our behalf. See Titus 2:13,14 where these words appear,

Our great God and Saviour, Jesus Christ, who gave himself for us to **redeem** us from all wickedness.

An example of the meaning of redemption is found in the history of the people of Israel. They were slaves in Egypt under hard taskmasters, but God delivered them. He redeemed them. God brought them out of Egyptian slavery with Moses as their leader. God's promise to Moses is found in Exodus 6:6:

> Therefore, say to the Israelites: 'I am the LORD, and I will bring you out from under the yoke of the Egyptians. I will **free you from being slaves** to them, and **I will redeem you** with an outstretched arm and with mighty acts of judgment.'

What God did for Israel in days of old, He has done for us who trust in His Son, Jesus Christ. Sin is no longer our master. We are no longer its slaves. We now have a new master, even God Himself. See this in Romans 6:22:

> You have been set free from sin and have become slaves to God.

Being a slave to God involves being a slave to righteousness, as Romans 6:18 puts it,

> You have been set free from sin and have become slaves to righteousness.

Christ has freed us from Sin

By His death and resurrection Christ has freed us from sin by redeeming us, so that we may now serve God and His righteousness. He paid the price of our freedom from sin and death. Becoming "slaves to righteousness" involves service to Him, and this should naturally follow the freedom we have been given. This will be considered more fully later.

Debtors: The Answer - Forgiveness

We are separated from God because we are debtors. The justice of God requires that sin shall be paid for by death. This we have already seen in the first part of Romans 6:23, "the wages of sin is death". As sinners we owe our lives to pay for sin - **we are in debt.**

By dying for our sins, Christ has paid this debt, so that we can now receive the forgiveness of sins. We could have no forgiveness apart from His death. See Hebrews 9:22:

> Without the shedding of blood there is no forgiveness.

The shedding of blood is a scriptural way of describing death and without Christ's death for us we could have no forgiveness. By His death He bore our sins. See 1 Peter 2:24. Speaking of Christ it says:

> He himself bore our sins in his body on the tree.

The tree in this verse is another way of speaking of the cross on which He died. He bore our sins so that we might have forgiveness. The debt has been paid and we are released from that debt. We are no longer debtors.

Summary so far

We have looked at the following aspects of our condition and God's remedy.

(1)   All are sinners because of their relationship to Adam.
(2)   Sinners are subject to death and separated from God.
(3)   Christ came into the world to save sinners.
(4)   He accepted the punishment for sin by His death and rose again from the dead.
(5)   When we believe in Him we are saved. We are saved by His life.

We also saw four aspects of the meaning of salvation under four headings:

(1)   Justification - God looks on us as though we are righteous.
(2)   Reconciliation - We are no longer enemies of God; peace has been made between us.

(3) Redemption - We are freed from being slaves to sin in order to serve God.

(4) Forgiveness - Our sins are forgiven; we are no longer debtors.

The Gift
of
Eternal Life

The Gift of Eternal Life

Romans 6:23 has been looked at before, but we have so far only considered the first part of the verse. The whole verse reads,

> For the wages of sin is death, but **the gift of God is eternal life** in Christ Jesus our Lord.

Eternal life is a gift from God that we accept by believing in Christ and trusting in His work for us. See John 3:16 again:

> For God so loved the world that he gave his one and only Son, that **whoever believes in him** shall not perish but have eternal life.

The opposite to eternal life is death (in Romans 6:23) and perishing (in John 3:16). There is no middle way; it is either life or death. This was so from the beginning.

In the Garden of Eden were two trees, the tree of life, and the tree of the knowledge of good and evil (Genesis 2:9; 3:22; 2:17). These trees represent the options – life and death.

> The tree of life ... **live for ever** (Genesis 3:22).

> The tree of the knowledge of good and evil ... (disobey and) ... **you will surely die** (Genesis 2:17).

| The choice! |
| Life or Death? |

Adam had the choice, life or death, dependent on his obedience to God. He chose disobedience and death. Each of us makes the same choice when faced with God's offer of salvation in Christ. We may choose to accept or reject Him, choose either life or death. Surely, we might say, nobody would consciously choose death, but this is not so. Consider John 5:39,40.

> You diligently study the Scriptures because you think that by them you possess eternal

life. These are the Scriptures that testify about me, yet you refuse to come to me to have life.

Here we have a group of Jews who knew the Scriptures well; they diligently studied them. But for all their knowledge they refused to come to the One who was the subject of those Scriptures, Christ himself. Of themselves the Scriptures cannot give life, but they point to Him who alone can give life. Reading this booklet cannot give eternal life. Neither can reading or studying the Bible, unless it leads us to believe in the One to whom it points. Life (or eternal life, the two are synonymous in John's Gospel) can only be found in Christ. These Jews were very learned men, who knew the Scriptures, but who refused to believe in the only One who could give them life. In verse 38 of this chapter we see that though they knew the word, it did not **dwell in them**. 1 John 5:11,12 puts it like this:

God has given us eternal life, and this life is in His Son. He who has the Son has life; he who does not have the Son of God does not have life.

Our relationship to Adam brings death. God has cancelled this death in Christ who gives life. By accepting Him as the One whom God gave, we accept the gift of eternal life in Him. Outside of Christ there is no life. His Word must be heard and/or read **and** believed. It must dwell in us.

The Judgment of God

We said earlier in this booklet, that God will not condemn a person for being a sinner because of their relationship to Adam. None of us can do anything about that. God judges a person by what they **choose**, when they either accept or reject Christ. If life can only be found in Him, then those who reject Him, reject the only way to life. In the world in which we live, life depends on light. If the sun's light were to be taken away, we would all die. Without light we could not live. This is why Christ is called in the Scriptures, "the light of the world".

When Jesus spoke again to the people, he said, 'I am the light of the world. Whoever follows me will never walk in darkness, but will have the light of life.' (John 8:12)

In order to have life it is necessary to receive the "light of the world", Christ; otherwise we remain in darkness and death. Once we realise that in Him only is life and light, then God will judge us according to whether or not we accept Him or reject Him. See John 3:18,19:

> Whoever believes in him is not condemned, but whoever does not believe stands condemned already because he has not believed in the name of God's one and only Son. This is the verdict: Light has come into the world, but men loved darkness instead of light because their deeds were evil.

People are condemned if they choose to remain in darkness when they know otherwise, by not coming to the Light and by not accepting Christ.

He alone is the Light and the source of life. **The judgement of God is based on response to light.** Where Christ is unknown there is the 'light' of the testimony of creation and the voice of conscience. But in large parts of the world today, Christ *is* preached, God's Word is available and His judgement will be based on that 'light'.

> [God] has set a day when he will judge the world with justice by the man he has appointed. He has given proof of this to all men by raising him from the dead. (Acts 12:31)

Where do we go from here?

We are now assuming that readers of this booklet have understood the need and provision of salvation in Christ. If not, we ask that before going any further, they will go back over what has been said and give it their earnest consideration. What follows is for those who have made a commitment, in that they have recognised their need of Christ and His work and accepted Him as their saviour.

The Meaning of Salvation for the Believer

The Meaning of Salvation for the Believer

a) A New Relationship

What does salvation mean to us now? As believers we have the assurance that we will be raised from the dead into a new and more wonderful life with Christ. We know little of that life, but are confident that it will be beyond anything we can now imagine. But this is future, what about now? What difference does being saved make to us now? Firstly we have **a new relationship** to God. See John 1:12:

> To all who received him (Christ), to those who believed in his name, he gave the right to become children of God.

| **Access to God is through Christ** | As children we enter into a relationship with God as our Father. Since God is our Father then we can approach Him as such. If we have problems or |

worries we can be confident that He will listen to us. Talking to God, either out loud or in our thoughts, is true prayer. Just as we thank an earthly father for what he does for us, so we should thank God for the blessings He gives us. All prayer should recognise that our access to God is **only possible through Christ** and it is essential to recognise this by praying in the name of Christ. See Ephesians 5:20:

> Giving thanks to God the Father for everything, in the name of our Lord Jesus Christ.

By asking our prayers "in the name of our Lord Jesus Christ" we remember all He has done for us and that it is through Him alone that we have access to God as our Father. None can approach or be with God the Father except through Him.

See John 14:6 where in response to Thomas' question, "How can we know the way?"

> Jesus answered, 'I am the way and the truth and the life. No-one comes to the Father except through me'.

b) Growing to Maturity

As our Father, God watches over us in a similar way to how any good earthly father watches over his children, but more so. He is concerned that we grow properly and has provided for our growth. The food that helps us grow to maturity, is the Word of God, the Bible or the Scriptures. Through the Bible we learn of God's ways and His purpose for us. We appreciate more of what it actually means to be a Christian and just how much we owe Christ. So we grow stronger in our faith and more able to give an answer to any who asks us why we have put our trust in Christ. We become more useful to God, and whilst we can never repay what He has done for us, by the witness of our lives we can give back just a little. The Scriptures prepare us for good works that must surely follow for any true believer. See 2 Timothy 3:16,17:

> All Scripture is God-breathed and is useful for teaching, rebuking, correcting and training in righteousness, so that the man of God may be thoroughly equipped for every good work.

Grow by feeding on God's Word

The expression, "man of God" suggests **growth** in the believer. We are not expected to remain like children, but to grow, just as we do in our physical lives. It is sad to see an adult with the mental age of a child; it is just as sad to see a believer who has never moved beyond the initial step of salvation and who has not grown spiritually as they have physically. The letter to the Hebrews has something to say about this. Complaining that the Hebrew believers were "slow to learn", the writer goes on to say,

Though by this time you ought to be teachers, you need someone to teach you the elementary truths of God's word all over again. You need milk, not solid food! Anyone who lives on milk, being still an infant, is not acquainted with the teaching about righteousness. But solid food is for the mature. (Hebrews 5:12-14)

Here were some believers who had not grown to maturity; they still needed milk like infants, being unable to take solid food. As new born Christians we start like infants with milk; the elementary things; the simple truth of faith in Christ, but we are expected to feed on God's Word and grow, preparing us for service to Him in good works. Through the Scriptures God speaks to us and guides us in our everyday lives, knowing more of Him and what he expects from us. For this we need solid food. We must grow.

c) Saved to Serve

When we are saved we begin a new life. This new life should be spent serving God by good works. We must be clear about this; good works **do not** save us, but having been saved by faith in Christ, we should then **serve God by good works**. See Ephesians 2:8-10 and notice in particular these words:

> It is by grace you have been saved, through faith …. Not by works … We are God's workmanship, created in Christ Jesus **to do good works**.

Here is the important difference between faith and good works,

> (1) Salvation comes to us **by** grace, **through** faith in Christ and based on **His** work
>
> (2) As His workmanship **we** are created **to do** good works

Our works cannot take the place of, or add to His grace, or our need of simple faith in Christ. But we are created for a purpose and once our relationship to God is put right through grace and faith, **then** we can fulfil that purpose by our good works. This was always God's intention and now through Christ, we are saved to serve Him.

d) Good Works and Service

Perhaps the most difficult thing for Christians to know is how they, as an individual, can serve God; how can they do good works? As we grow as believers, through reading and absorbing God's Word, and become more mature, God may call us to serve Him in one particular way, but we do not have to wait for this day to come, for we can serve Him now. Service is firstly the kind of life we lead. The Scriptures list various types of good works, all of them common sense and many of them probably already part of our everyday lives. Here are a few.

Love to others

See 1 John 4:7-11 and notice especially verse 11:

> Since God so loved us, we also ought to love one another.

God's great love was shown to us when He gave His Son to pay for our sins. This is the greatest love that any can give. John 15:13:

> Greater love has no-one than this, that he lay down his life for his friends.

His love was shown by **giving**. We may serve God by our love to others and giving will form a large part of it. Philippians 2:4 tells us what 'giving' means for the believer when it says,

> Each of you should look not only to your own interests, but also to **the interests of others**.

Following Christ's example We are not told to neglect our own things, but to have consideration also for others. In the passage from Philippians quoted above, the example of Christ is given, who descended from His exalted position and thought and acted like a servant for the sake of others. (See 2:5-8.) It is this attitude of mind we are asked to follow. His concern for us should inspire in us a concern for others. This loving and giving is Christian service and will involve good works.

Forgiveness

See Ephesians 4:32

> Be kind and compassionate to one another, forgiving each other, just as in Christ God forgave you.

Again we are to follow an example, this time of God's forgiveness in Christ. He has forgiven us all our sins against Himself, and so ought we to forgive those who sin against us. This may not be easy at times, but we should remember that it was not easy for God either. His Son suffered for us and went through the death of the cross for our forgiveness. Surely we can forgive and forget the wrongs done to us when we think of His example.

Our conversation

When we believe in Christ we need to be careful in both our words and actions, especially in what we say. It is very easy to speak out without thinking or in a moment of anger. Once something is said it cannot be withdrawn, so we must be careful. If we can control our tongue we are able to control all that we do. See James 3:2

> If anyone is never at fault in what he says, he is a perfect man, able to keep his whole body in check.

Words are so important; wars have started over them. We must control our tongues. See the following verses in Ephesians 4:25-31:

> Each of you must put off falsehood and speak truthfully to his neighbour. (verse 25)

> Do not let any unwholesome talk come out of your mouths, but only what is helpful for building others up according to their needs,

that it may benefit those who listen. (verse 29)

Get rid of all bitterness, rage and anger, brawling and slander, along with every form of malice. (verse 31)

As believers we should always speak the truth, never falsely or in anger or bitterness, but always in kindness and love. What we say and how we say it are of great importance. Again we have the example of Christ to follow. See 1 Peter 2:21-23:

Christ suffered for you, leaving you an example, that you should follow in His steps. He committed no sin, and no deceit was found in His mouth. When they hurled their insults at him, he did not retaliate; when he suffered, he made no threats.

Others spoke against Him, accusing Him of things He had never done, but He never retaliated, He never insulted them. We should do likewise, not only when others speak against us, but always. See Colossians 4:6:

Let your conversation be always full of grace, seasoned with salt, so that you may know how to answer every one.

By our conversation we can show to others something of the grace of God that has made so much difference to our lives, and perhaps bring them also to appreciate the great salvation we have in Christ.

Obedience

We tend to think that this word is confined to children, and indeed the Bible does apply it in this way when it says, "Children, obey your parents in everything, for this pleases the Lord" (Colossians 3:20). It has always been right for young persons to give honour to their mothers and fathers. This was one of the Ten Commandments given to the Jews (see Exodus 20:12). This honour is shown by obedience, and the Lord is pleased with such, and gives His blessing.

The Bible warns us of a time when there will be disobedience to parents (2 Tim. 3:2), and we seem to be already living in these days and reaping the consequences of it. Young believers may show their love to God by their love to their parents, and obedience plays a big part in this. Jesus Christ is again the example to follow, for He was obedient to Joseph and Mary when a young man of twelve years (Luke 2: 40-51).

But obedience is not confined to the young; disobedience was in fact the beginning of all mankind's troubles. Of Adam, an adult, it is written in Romans 5:19,

> Through the **disobedience** of the one man the many were made sinners.

Adam is here contrasted with Christ, who was obedient to His Father. Romans 5:19 goes on to say,

> Through the **obedience** of the one man the many will be made righteous.

He obeyed His Father in Heaven when He gave up His life for us. See Philippians 2:8:

> Being found in appearance as a man, he humbled himself and became obedient to death - even death on a cross!

Obedience begins when we are young, but is just as much a part of the adult Christian life. It is relevant to all ages and all times.

As He is

The words of this heading are taken from 1 John 3:2:

> Now we are children of God, and what we will be has not yet been made known. But we know that when he appears, we shall be like Him, for we shall see him **as he is**.

Our hope is to be like Him; Christ-like, and one day we shall be. We shall be as He is. When man was first created, he was like God in one particular way. See Genesis 1:26,27:

Then God said, 'Let us make man in our image, in our likeness' ... So God created man in his own image, in the image of God he created him.

When Adam fell (under the influence of Satan) he became a sinner, and his likeness to God was spoilt. The coming of sin into the world interfered with the purpose of God for man, and made necessary the death of Christ to undo this work of the devil. See the second part of 1 John 3:8:

The reason the Son of God appeared was to destroy the devil's work.

See also verse 5 of the same chapter:

He appeared so that he might take away our sins.

Like Him then, like Him now

Christ came to destroy the devil and his works, to take away our sins and make it possible for us to be like Him. This is one of the reasons we have been saved, so as to be like Him. But this is yet future, how should this influence us now? God desires that even now, in everyday life, we should strive to be like Him. See 1 John 3:2,3:

> When he appears, we shall be like him … Everyone who has this hope in him purifies himself, just as he is pure.

The word pure in this context means separated from sin. God, through Christ, has delivered us from sin and we should now avoid it in everyday life. We still have to live in a world where there is much evil, and we will be tempted to sin from time to time, but God knows this and gives us the strength to resist. Christ prayed for His disciples in John 17:15, not that they should be either immune from or kept away from temptation, but **protected**:

> My prayer is not that you take them out of the world but that you protect them from the evil one.

We also have the assurance of the words of 1 Corinthians 10:13:

> No temptation has seized you except what is common to man. And God is faithful; he will not let you be tempted beyond what you can bear. But when you are tempted, he will also provide a way out so that you can stand up under it.

As a Christian, striving to follow the example of Christ, trying to be like Him, we may be subjected to many temptations. But God knows us better than we know ourselves. He knows our weaknesses and makes allowances.

> As a father has compassion on his children, so the Lord has compassion on those who fear him; for he knows how we are formed, he remembers that we are dust. (Psalm 103:13,14)

God's tests

All things that are of any worth have been tested or tried. So it is with the Christian. Some tests may be unpleasant, but they are necessary. God may use circumstances to test us, allowing situations to take their course so as to test us, to find out our worth and to examine our faith in Him. Tests are really for our benefit of course, for God knows beforehand how we will react under any circumstances, and He is well pleased when our faith is not shaken. Why does He test us? See firstly the word of God to Israel in Deuteronomy 8:2,3.

> Remember how the LORD your God led you all the way in the desert these forty years, to humble you and to test you **in order to know what was in your heart**, whether or not you would keep his commands. He humbled you, causing you to hunger and then feeding you.

When in the wilderness, Israel suffered a shortage of food common to such environments.

They were kept waiting, before God supplied their need. This was a test to see whether or not they would trust Him. But instead of believing in the One who had so wonderfully brought them out of the slavery of Egypt, they murmured against Him - their faith failed. They should have known that God, having saved them, would not allow them to starve in the wilderness.

So God may test us, not necessarily as in the example of Israel, but He may well keep us waiting, to test our faith. This could be true of our prayers. God does not always answer prayer straight away, but may delay the answer, or even say no, to test our desire and our faith in Him.

We may also be tested by the circumstances through which He allows us to pass. Life is not always easy. Sometimes we have difficulties and troubles; things happen which depress and sadden us, or somebody is unwell and we begin to worry. Sometimes we wonder why God allows such things to happen at all - why do good people suffer, and bad people prosper? We may even suffer at the hands of others because of what we believe.

In ages past believers have been ill-treated simply for being believers, often being wrongly accused, persecuted or just mocked. It is possible that we may find ourselves in similar circumstances, but whatever happens, we should look upon it as a **test** of our faith in God. He is not of course responsible for how we are treated by others, which is down to them, but is concerned how we react to our circumstances. In this way He examines our faith and trust in Him. Peter wrote to some believers who were passing through a testing time in I Peter 1:6,7:

> Now for a little while you may have had to suffer grief in all kinds of trials. These have come so that your faith – of greater worth than gold, which perishes even though refined by fire – may be proved genuine.

God allowed the faith of these believers to be tested, and He may do the same to each of us, although not necessarily in the same way. May we always trust Him whatever comes and however unpleasant the test.

God's discipline

A wise and loving father will correct his children when they go wrong. He disciplines them because he wants them to take the right path in life and be happy. So God, as our Father, may correct us, but it is an evidence of His love for us and our relationship to Him. See Hebrews 12:6:

> The Lord disciplines those he loves, and he punishes everyone he accepts as a son.

God may use some of the trials of life, mentioned above under God's tests, to discipline us. It may not be pleasant at the time, but He desires only our good, and one day we will look back and thank Him for the way He has led us. See Hebrews 12:11:

> No discipline seems pleasant at the time, but painful. Later on, however, it produces

a harvest of righteousness and peace for those who have been trained by it.

The discipline of the Lord is for our good, even though at the time it may be unpleasant. The future will show God's great wisdom in dealing with us so, even though we do not at present understand why. Trust Him now and the future will reveal all. Touched by the salvation of God, we may be asked to pass through trying times and unpleasant circumstances, but we may be sure that He will not forget us or desert us. Always He plans for our good. He is not taken by surprise by anything that either His great enemy Satan or sinful men may do. He is able to work all things, whether good or evil, for good. See Romans 8:28:

> We know that in all things God works for the good of those who love him, who have been called according to His purpose.

All things are in His hands, and if He is for us, who can be against us? (See Romans 8:31.)

A Summary of what Salvation means for us as Believers

A Summary of what Salvation means for us as Believers

(1) We have **a new relationship to God**. He is our Father and we His children. We should go to Him in prayer, thanking Him for all things, telling Him our worries and problems. We can approach Him only through Jesus Christ. He speaks to us through His word, the Bible, which we should read regularly. By His word we are prepared to serve Him.

(2) We have been **saved to serve Him** by good works. The life we lead is service for Him when we are loving, kind, forgiving, obedient, etc. We should be careful in our conversation and all that we do should be done for Him.

(3) We should **seek to be like Him**, especially avoiding sin. We live in a sinful world, but just as He was able to live in that world without

sharing in its sinful ways, so should we avoid all sin. We may be tempted to sin, but He will help at all times.

(4) We will have **times of testing**, but God, like any father, is concerned about His children. He allows us to be tested by circumstances and seeks our trust in Him at such times. He may also **discipline us for our own good,** even though it may not be pleasant at the time. He is in complete control and works all things together for good. In Christ we have the certainty that as God is for us, it matters not who is against us.

Conclusion

Conclusion

Salvation includes all that is written in this booklet and very much more. At present we see only a part of what salvation means for us now, and will mean in the future. One day we shall know even more about God's great salvation in Christ Jesus. Until then we should never cease to thank Him for what He has done for us, for the gift of His Son, and all that comes to us through Him. Romans 8:31,32 tells of the confidence we should have because of the position we have in Christ. It needs no comment, for it speaks for itself:

> What then, shall we say in response to this? If God is for us, who can be against us? He who did not spare his own Son, but gave him up for us all - how will he not also, along with him, graciously give us all things?

If God is for us, who can be against us? This booklet was not written simply for interest but to challenge all who read it. If we call ourselves Christians, what right have we to do this? Many who live in civilised countries call themselves by the name 'Christian', but are they Christians as defined by the Word of God, the Bible?

A Christian **IS NOT** a person who,

> Lives in a civilised country.
> Goes to, or is a member of, a Church.
> Lives the best life they can.
> Is christened, baptised and/or confirmed.
> Knows the Bible from back to front.

A Christian **IS** one who

> Believes in Jesus Christ as their Saviour – and the five things listed above are secondary to this basic truth.

Are you a believer? It is easy to say that we believe in Christ as our Saviour, but if we do, it should make a difference in our lives. A person who really believes in Him has new life; they start all over again like a new-born baby. They think differently than they did before and now have new interests. They will want to spend time with God by reading His word, praying, and meeting with others who also believe in the Lord Jesus Christ. Their life should be lived for the Lord who has saved them, and not selfishly. They have life, and they have it more abundantly. Are you like this?

Before you put this booklet to one side ask yourself where you stand, and be sure to answer honestly. Remember that "*now* is the time of God's favour, *now* is the day of salvation" (2 Corinthians 6:2).

Appendix

Those who have never heard of Jesus Christ

Appendix

Those who have never heard of Jesus Christ

We are well aware that insisting there is no salvation apart from the work of Christ poses a problem. The great majority of those who have lived and died on this earth have never even heard of Him, let alone had the opportunity to believe in Him. This is a subject beyond the brief of this booklet, but how will God judge this great multitude? The most that can be said here, on the basis of Scriptural teaching, is that God has never left Himself without a witness in any age, in so far that mankind has

1) the witness of creation, and
2) the voice of conscience.

God, who knows the minds and hearts, is well able to judge from man's response to these evidences, to know how an individual *would have reacted* to the preaching of salvation, had they had that opportunity. See Romans 1:20; 2:14-16.

More on Salvation

Salvation: Safe and Secure
By Sylvia Penny

This is a thorough treatment of the subject of salvation, asking such questions as …

- What is it, exactly, that saves us?
- Who is saved?
- Is salvation secure?
- Can it be lost?
- What is 'conditional security'?

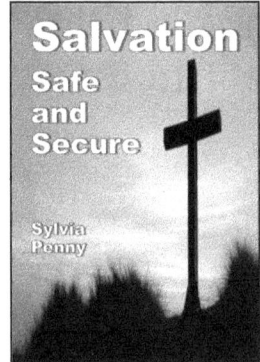

It deals with a wide number of issues such as …

- Salvation and works
- The doctrine of rewards
- Lordship salvation
- Free grace theology
- Assurance of salvation
- Why people lose their faith

God's Gift of Everlasting Life
By William Campbell

Taking his authority as the Bible, the author deals with a wide range of subjects relating to death and eternal life. Such as:

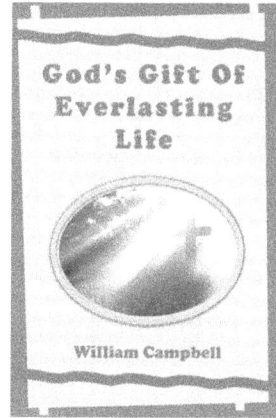

· Who possess immortality?
· What is the soul, and is it immortal?
· What is the spirit, and is it immortal?
· Is man body, soul and spirit?
· What happens at death?
· What are sheol and hades?
· What happens at resurrection?
· What happens to unbelievers?
· And many more.

A well written, thorough, and easy to read book based solely on Scripture.

Seven Aspects of Salvation
By Brian Sherring

In short, but comprehensive, coverage Brian Sherring gives the reader a greater understanding of 'salvation'. We may often use the word 'saved', but having been 'saved' do we appreciate many of the other gracious blessings that goes along with it, such as:

- Identification with Christ
- Reconciliation
- Redemption
- Justification
- Atonement
- Sanctification
- Eternal Life

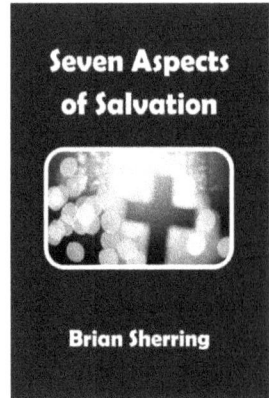

And, with respect to salvation, what is the role of the New Covenant;

    (a) with respect to Israel, and
    (b) with respect to the Church the Body of Christ?

Further details of these books,
and the ones on other pages,
can be seen on **www.obt.org**

They can all be ordered from that
website and also from

The Open Bible Trust
Fordland Mount, Upper Basildon,
Reading, RG8 8LU, UK.

They are also all available as eBooks
from Amazon and Apple
and as KDP paperbacks from Amazon.

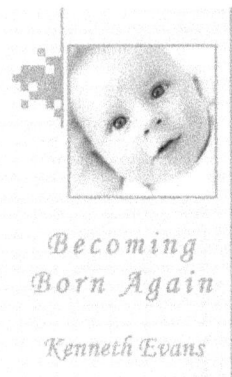

That Wonderful Redemption
By Athol Walter

God's Work of Salvation
By Vicky Wilkinson

Becoming Born Again
Kenneth Evans

Life in Christ
By William Campbell

This excellent book is a comprehensive treatment of the biblical truth that immortality is only for those who have faith in Christ and that they are given this at the second advent of Christ.

It is a course of twenty three lessons split into five parts as follows:

- Part 1: The Human Body
- Part 2: The Soul
- Part 3: The Spirit
- Part 4: Death
- Part 5: Resurrection

No words can describe the entrancing prospect of being raised and given eternal life when Christ returns. That was the goal for which the Lord Jesus Christ, God's beloved Son, came and died for us, shed His life's blood, and rose again. And just as He rose and has a glorious resurrection body, so will we.

About the author

Brian Sherring was born in Isleworth, Middlesex, England in 1932. Following a technical education, he took an engineering apprenticeship and worked for some years as a design draughtsman in agricultural engineering. He was one time Assistant Principal of The Chapel of the Opened Book in London and wrote for The Berean Expositor but now writes for *Search* magazine. He now lives with his wife in retirement in Surrey.

He has written a number of major books including:

The Ten Commandments
Messiah and His People
The Mystery of Ephesians
Romans: Background and Introduction

Details can be seen on **www.obt.org.uk**

Brian Sherring is a regular contributor to
Search magazine

For a free sample of
The Open Bible Trust's magazine Search,
please email

admin@obt.org.uk

or visit

www.obt.org.uk/search

Also by Brian Sherring

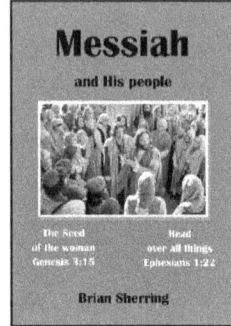

Paul's Letter to the Romans: Background & Introduction

This book sets Paul's letter to the Romans in the context of both the New Testament and his other letters. It gives the reader a good basis for a detailed study of the epistle.

It was written from Greece some three years before Paul arrived in Rome (Acts 20:2-3). This means that it was written *before* the judgement Paul pronounced upon the Jewish leaders in Rome (Acts 28:25-28). That is *before* Paul wrote Ephesians and Colossians in which new teachings are revealed about a heavenly calling, about Gentile and Jewish equality, and about the abolishment of the Law of Moses. It is essential when reading Romans, not to read back into it such teaching as these, and the author does an excellent job of explaining Romans in its correct historical context.

The Mystery of Ephesians

In Ephesians 3:3 Paul mentions a 'mystery', and states that he had written about it briefly, i.e. earlier in the letter. So ... What is this 'mystery'? ... Why have so few Christians heard about it? ... And why do some, who have heard about it, reject it? ... Even oppose it?

With great clarity Brian Sherring explains the Greek word   translated 'mystery' does not mean something 'mysterious' but refers to a 'secret', and this 'secret' is an important one. It relates to all mankind, and God had just revealed it to Paul and wanted Paul to make it known far and wide ... which is just what he did in writing Ephesians.

Messiah and His People

In this book Brian Sherring takes the reader through the Bible and the unfolding portrait it paints of the Messiah, the Christ, the Redeemer.

He starts off in Genesis 3, where we learn of the seed of the woman who is to crush the serpent's head, and as we progress through time, slowly more and more is revealed about this One. He is to descend from Abraham and be of the house of David. He is to be born of a virgin and be born in Bethlehem.

He is to combine the offices of Prophet, Priest and King. From Ephesians 1 we learn that in the end He is to be head over all things and Philippians 2 states He is to have that Name which is above every name.

Apocalypse
An Introduction to
Revelation

This is simply one of the best, if not *the* best, introduction to the Book of Revelation.

Revelation! A book that fascinates some Christians, but one that confuses others.

How can we start making sense of Revelation? Read this booklet. It will help you no end. It is not a detailed study which will bog you down. Rather it provides some keys that will unlock the last book of the Bible and enable Christians to begin to understand it and get it into perspective.

****

These books can be ordered from
www.obt.org.uk

They are also all available as eBooks from
Amazon and Apple
and as KDP paperbacks from Amazon.

About this book

Salvation

God's Provision and our Response

Salvation is not a word that is much used in everyday speech, but from its earliest chapters the Bible speaks of man's need for *salvation*, and from then onwards, it runs through the Bible from beginning to end. Man may need salvation, but it is God who provides it.

This book is not a theological treatise and considers the basic truth of *salvation* to be enshrined in the words, "Believe in the Lord Jesus, and you shall be saved" (Acts 16:31). With that as his starting point, the author looks at *salvation* from a number of angles so that the reader will see that *salvation* is the most vital truth for people to understand and take hold of.

Publications of The Open Bible Trust must be in accordance with its evangelical, fundamental and dispensational basis. However, beyond this minimum, writers are free to express whatever beliefs they may have as their own understanding, provided that the aim in so doing is to further the object of The Open Bible Trust. A copy of the doctrinal basis is available on **www.obt.org.uk** or from:

THE OPEN BIBLE TRUST
Fordland Mount, Upper Basildon,
Reading, RG8 8LU, GB